Eati

CW01664583

Disorders

Guidance for Teachers

Christine Lewis BSc
Amanda Johnson BA, RGN
Nicholas Lewis BA, PGCE

Family Reading Centre

Published in the United Kingdom by:
Family Reading Centre Ltd
126 Sutherland Avenue, Biggin Hill
Kent TN16 3HJ

Copyright © 1994 Christine Lewis, Amanda Johnson
and Nicholas Lewis

First published June 1994

All rights reserved.
No part of this publication may be reproduced or transmitted, in any form or by any means, electronic or mechanical, including photocopy, recording or any information storage and retrieval system, without permission in writing from the publisher.

A catalogue record for this booklet
is available from the British Library

ISBN 1-898538-O2-6

Edited, designed and typeset in the UK by:
Life Skills Training Services, 163 Clifton Road
Rugby, Warwickshire CV21 3QN

Printed in the UK by Impressions Printing Technology, Sevenoaks
Kent TN14 5HD

Introduction

Research has shown that two per cent of girls and young women suffer from anorexia or bulimia. Of these, 10 per cent die through starvation or suicide. Compulsive eating is another serious disorder. The social and psychological effects of being overweight, together with the shame of bingeing, are difficult for any child. It is important, therefore, that these conditions are diagnosed early so that treatment can begin as soon as possible.

Teachers are strategically placed to recognise potential problems

Boys and young men also have eating disorders, but this is much less frequent.

Teachers are strategically placed to recognise potential problems. Those with pastoral roles have a vital part to play in supporting the student as he or she seeks and undergoes treatment.

This booklet has been produced with secondary school teachers in mind. The problem of eating disorders, however, often emerges much earlier. Since prevention is better than cure, it is important for **primary school teachers** also to familiarise themselves with the causes and symptoms of eating disorders.

We live in a fashion-conscious, weight-conscious and diet-conscious society. Children and teenagers, as well as adults, are putting a lot of energy into efforts to achieve physical perfection. In addition to idolising *appearance,* many families idolise *performance.* They make approval and affection conditional. Children in other families suffer verbal, emotional or physical abuse.

An eating disorder is the physical expression of emotional distress. Increasingly, it is becoming a response to the external and internal pressures experienced by young people today. It is an addictive behaviour pattern. The person has a compulsion to use the 'drug' of her choice - food or starvation - to suppress feelings rather than face and express them.

Children in the eight- to ten-year age range are exhibiting symptoms of anorexia that require hospital treatment

A girl may become preoccupied with food and weight as a way of coping with unresolved stress and the difficulties of everyday living. The eating disorder becomes the 'solution' to the underlying problems. The person with an eating disorder believes she has control over her life. The truth is, she is damaging both herself and those around her.

There is much that schools can do to help prevent young people from developing eating disorders, as well as to help those already affected by them. They can incorporate material on self-esteem, body image, and male and female stereotyping into lesson plans. Ideally, **this needs to begin at primary school level.** Children in the eight- to ten-year age range are exhibiting symptoms of anorexia that require hospital treatment.

Teachers may well notice signs of anorexia or compulsive eating, although bulimia is more difficult to spot. It is important to understand that these disorders may overlap or occur one after the other. A compulsive eater, for instance, may become overweight in early teens, go on a rigorous diet leading to anorexia, then find bulimia an easier way of coping.

It is essential that referrals are made quickly through the school's pastoral structure

It is essential that referrals are made quickly through the school's pastoral structure. Early medical diagnosis and close co-operation between school, family and others will ensure that pastoral staff can make the best contribution to a young person's recovery.

In this booklet the feminine pronoun has been used for a person with an eating disorder. 'He' or 'his' should be substituted by the reader who is considering the less usual case of a boy or young man with eating problems.

About the authors

Christine Lewis has a degree in nutrition from London University and a diploma in counselling from Waverley Abbey Christian Training Centre, Farnham, Hampshire. She is the author of *The Food Choice Jungle* and a number of booklets. She has been working in the field of eating disorders for a number of years.

Amanda Johnson is a qualified nurse who now works as a youth worker and counsellor for a large church in Norwich. She has worked with children and young people in a variety of settings. As part of a recent degree course she carried out practical work and desk research on helping people with eating disorders.

Nicholas Lewis is a form tutor in a comprehensive school in Guildford, Surrey. He has a special interest in the pastoral care of young people.

Note

Throughout this booklet the following simplifications are used:

anorexia - for anorexia nervosa
bulimia - for bulimia nervosa
compulsive eating - for binge eating disorder

Index

Compulsive eating: Food hunger or hunger for love?

> The compulsive eater is addicted to food in much the same way as an alcoholic is addicted to alcohol or a workaholic to work

Compulsive eaters are people who eat to satisfy emotional hunger, of which they may not be aware. The compulsive eater may be very overweight, but this is not the real issue. More important are the *reasons* for compulsive eating.

The compulsive eater is addicted to food in much the same way as an alcoholic is addicted to alcohol or a workaholic to work. This strong emotional reliance on something external makes the person feel good on the inside. Unless the underlying issues for the behaviour are identified, the person will never be free from her compulsive relationship with food.

Eleven-year-old Janine has always been encouraged to eat a lot at home. Now, when the going gets tough, she automatically finds comfort in the fridge. Recently, she has felt rejected by some of her classmates at the new school. She blots out her feelings of rejection by eating as much as she can get hold of. Janine is a *compulsive eater* who nurtures and protects herself by overeating.

Common reasons for compulsive eating

- ❒ Response to cultural pressure
- ❒ Subconscious desire to add weight as protection from love and intimacy
- ❒ Using food to satisfy the need for immediate gratification
- ❒ Using food as a tranquilliser
- ❒ Focusing on the desire for food to avoid facing problems
- ❒ Eating to punish self or others
- ❒ Eating to relieve depression or stress
- ❒ Eating to rebel against self or others
- ❒ Eating to express the need to control circumstances
- ❒ Faulty perception of body image
- ❒ Emotional feelings about food that were developed during early childhood
- ❒ Using food as a nurturer to satisfy a hunger for love

The compulsive eater uses food as a nurturer to satisfy a hunger for love

Underlying issues

- ❒ Longing to be loved
- ❒ Negative feelings
- ❒ Sense of loss, loneliness, emptiness
- ❒ Disappointment in relationships
- ❒ Denial
- ❒ Eating to mask emotional problems
- ❒ Food being used as a tranquilliser
- ❒ Seeing fatness as a means of self-protection - being overweight can be blamed for any rejection
- ❒ Fear of being slim and sexually attractive

Anorexia: The slimmer's disease?

Anorexia was originally defined as 'appetite loss of nervous origin'. There is more to anorexia than 'nerves', however, because the physiological changes resulting from the disorder cause further problems. Also, the anorexic has usually *conquered* her appetite rather than *lost* it.

There is more to anorexia than 'nerves'; the anorexic has usually *conquered* her appetite rather than *lost* it

The nickname 'slimmer's disease' is also misleading. It doesn't take into account the underlying psychological problems that go with the desire to be thin. In some cases this includes wanting to have a child-like body to avoid facing adulthood.

Annette is 13 and has just been diagnosed as having *anorexia.* She is concerned about how she looks, and she often talks about being overweight even though she is incredibly thin. She tends to eat on her own at home so that no one can see how little she is taking in. At school she often makes excuses for not going to lunch: 'I've got to get that piece on the piano just right.' 'I'm training on my own in the gym.' Annette's periods haven't begun yet but, as with other areas of her secretive life, she pretends to her friends that everything is perfectly normal.

Signs and symptoms

Some of these may be seen, while others remain hidden. It is important that the person is diagnosed by a doctor, since her weight loss may be due to some underlying illness.

It is important that the person suspected of anorexia is diagnosed by a doctor, since her weight loss may be due to some underlying illness

- ❒ Active refusal to eat enough to maintain normal weight, or vomiting, or purging with laxatives
- ❒ Severe weight loss
- ❒ Loss of menstrual periods for at least three months, or very light, irregular periods for six months
- ❒ Excessive concern over appearance, with fear of weight gain
- ❒ Excessive exercise in an effort to control weight
- ❒ Avoidance of 'fattening' foods
- ❒ Denial of hunger
- ❒ Skipping lunch at school
- ❒ Hiding or discarding food
- ❒ Obsessive interest in calories, weight and body shape
- ❒ Need to eat alone, unobserved
- ❒ Emotional and irritable behaviour, indecisiveness, apathy, depression
- ❒ Possible change in personality
- ❒ Adopting black-or-white thinking and attitudes
- ❒ Arranging rigid and inflexible routines for work and exercise
- ❒ Perfectionism - reworking material over and over again
- ❒ Becoming aggressive and manipulative
- ❒ Increasing isolation
- ❒ Loss of close friends

- ❒ Switching from team sport to solitary sport
- ❒ Insomnia
- ❒ Feeling the cold
- ❒ Growth of downy hair on the body

Underlying issues

> Underlying anorexia is a conflict between wanting independence and the need to be dependent

- ❒ Longing for love
- ❒ Low self-worth
- ❒ Perfectionism
- ❒ Negative feelings
- ❒ Desire to be in control
- ❒ Denial
- ❒ Distorted view of body image
- ❒ Intense fear of gaining weight
- ❒ Intense fear of rejection
- ❒ Conflict between wanting independence and the need to be dependent
- ❒ Identity crisis
- ❒ Fear of sexuality

Medical dangers

- ❒ Early osteoporosis ('brittle bones')
- ❒ Slow heartbeat
- ❒ Lethargy
- ❒ Damage to reproductive organs
- ❒ Fluid retention
- ❒ Kidney problems
- ❒ Possibility of suicidal thoughts

Bulimia: A way of coping with life?

Bulimia means 'ox-like hunger', or voracious appetite. It was first diagnosed in 1979, but the habit of bingeing and vomiting or purging with laxatives has been recorded for thousands of years.

Bingeing usually involves eating exceptionally large amounts of high-calorie foods in a comparatively short period of time. This generally happens in response to negative feelings of anger, anxiety or shame caused by what the person tells herself about a given situation or set of circumstances. In some cases there are physical factors involved. One such is food sensitivity, in which eating a specific food, such as chocolate, seems to be a powerful trigger. Another is premenstrual syndrome giving rise to sugar-craving.

Bingeing generally happens in response to negative feelings of anger, anxiety or shame caused by what the person tells herself about a given situation

Bingeing can bring the person to the point of sedation, thus warding off sexual feelings. It can also be used to ease a sense of loss in a relationship. By eating enormous amounts, the person is saying, 'I'm desperately needy.' Then, by purging herself through starvation, vomiting, laxatives or diuretics (medicines to aid the discharge of urine), she is saying, 'I reject it all. I don't deserve anything.'

Two episodes of bingeing and purging a week for three months is one of the criteria for diagnosis. Bulimics can be of normal weight, or they can be under- or overweight.

Catlyn is 16 and was slightly overweight until she was 12. Within a few months of dieting, she had become emaciated. Soon she was diagnosed and treated for anorexia. For three years she managed to eat fairly normally. Then she began comfort eating and making herself sick afterwards. Friends and family often comment on how much she can eat without putting on any weight. She keeps it all hushed up, but the truth is that her former anorexia - which everyone thinks was cured - has now turned into *bulimia.*

Often the bulimic makes every effort to keep signs and symptoms of their disorder hidden

Signs and symptoms

A teacher may observe some of these, but often the bulimic makes every effort to keep them hidden:

- ❒ Recurrent episodes of uncontrollable eating
- ❒ Devious and deceptive behaviour
- ❒ Repeated attempts to lose weight
- ❒ Vigorous exercise and dieting
- ❒ Sore throat and erosion of tooth enamel due to vomiting
- ❒ Menstrual disturbances
- ❒ Dehydration and poor skin condition
- ❒ Intense desire to look good and be in control
- ❒ Dramatic extrovert behaviour
- ❒ Making close friends, being demanding, then dropping them

- ❒ Seeking help, then rejecting it
- ❒ Multi-impulsive antisocial behaviour in addition to bulimia: alcohol or drug abuse, stealing money for binges, lying, promiscuous sexual activity

Underlying issues

- ❒ Longing to be loved
- ❒ Low self-worth
- ❒ Negative feelings
- ❒ Desiring control and independence yet feeling helpless and wanting to be dependent
- ❒ Conflict
- ❒ Mixed feelings towards food, relationships and recovery
- ❒ Misuse of sexuality
- ❒ Denial
- ❒ Fear of discovery and rejection

Underlying bulimia are mixed feelings towards food, relationships and recovery

Medical dangers

- ❒ Excessive biochemical imbalances that could lead to life-threatening heart problems
- ❒ Permanent damage to teeth
- ❒ Damage to the oesophagus (digestive tract between mouth and stomach)

Issues beneath the surface of eating disorders

The causes of compulsive eating, anorexia and bulimia are very complex, and each condition arises from the person's whole life experience. Certain contributing factors and areas of need can be highlighted because they are often seen:

Insecurity

The person is driven by fear of failure and rejection. As a result, she concentrates all her energies around food and eating. As a form of self-protection she avoids socialising and stays in a world of unreality. The bulimic is torn between wanting to be loved and being afraid of rejection.

The person with an eating disorder is driven by fear of failure and rejection

Low self-worth and longing for love

Feeling helpless and wanting to be rescued are often driving factors for both anorexics and bulimics, though they are unable to recognise this. They are searching for *unconditional love,* to be accepted for who they are rather than for their achievements or how they look. They can't express love effectively. They believe they are worthless and deserving punishment, so they are prone to depression.

The anorexic's desire for approval leads to perfectionism and rigorous self-discipline. She sees loss of control as a failure. As a result, she often appears as the perfect daughter, submissive and helpful. She believes she has to live by unrealistic standards set by others and by the media. In this way she sets herself up to fail.

Identity crisis

Because she wants to live up to other people's expectations, she has difficulty knowing who she really is. She is uncertain how much of herself is moulded by others and where she stands in relation to them. The anorexic, fearing that other people are trying to control her, uses her eating disorder as a way of exerting control over her own body. The bulimic has a conflict between wanting to be independent and the fear of actually being so.

The anorexic, fearing that other people are trying to control her, uses her eating disorder as a way of exerting control over her own body

Sexuality struggles

The anorexic holds back from accepting herself as a woman. The bulimic struggles between wanting to express her femininity and believing she is despicable and unworthy of love. This conflict about sexuality may be related to present conflicts or to past hurts such as rejection or sexual abuse.

Issues related to decreased weight

Effects on the mind

Long-term starvation has effects of which the girl is unaware. Starvation affects her mind as well as her body. Her thinking is restricted; the lower her weight goes, the smaller the range of things she is likely to think about.

She has polarised thinking, and her values become rigid and absolute. Everything is good or bad, black or white, acceptable or unacceptable. She sees everything of importance in terms of food, though good academic progress can mask this for a while.

> Long-term starvation has effects of which the girl is unaware. The lower her weight goes, the smaller the range of things she is likely to think about

The chart on page 20 shows changes occurring as a person's weight drops.

Effects on school work

In subjects such as languages, the able student with an eating disorder will continue to get high marks for some time if she puts in long hours at repetitive learning. In this way she masks her inability to think in abstract terms or to think creatively.

Changes occurring as weight falls

Approaching 80% body weight	Thinking changes	Appearance is often good
Around 80%	Menstruation is impaired	Appearance of being anorexic is not obvious
75-70%	Thinking becomes even more polarised and rigid	Looks frail
65%	If weight is falling at 3-4 pounds a week, this is medically dangerous	
65-60%	The person becomes accident-prone and should not drive a car	
60%	Definitely medically dangerous	

Gradually, in subjects needing problem-solving or creative organisation of ideas, her diminished intellectual capacity will cause her difficulties. For example, when weight is down to 85 per cent of the acceptable norm, a person studying A-level mathematics is likely to get lower marks.

As weight falls even lower, a student begins to be affected in other ways:

- ❒ Less able to take in new information
- ❒ Less able to write essays or letters
- ❒ Unable to work in groups because too many interactions overwhelm her
- ❒ Has difficulty being spontaneous and flexible with people
- ❒ Chooses isolation

Exercise and sport

The highest incidence of anorexia occurs in schools and colleges of sport, dance, drama and modelling

Success in sport is equated with excellence and is admired in education, industry and government.

Many people depend on being in control over food and exercise to gain a sense of self-worth. This is often the case with anorexics and bulimics. Most anorexics have always been good at sport and are very committed to it. The highest incidence of anorexia occurs in schools and colleges of sport, dance, drama and modelling.

Hunger induces restlessness and insomnia, so a girl may get up at five in the morning to go running. Such hyperactivity may be confused with commitment. It is well known that exercising to excess causes changes in brain chemistry, inducing feelings of well-being and success. Exercise addiction is a recognised condition. In it, exercise becomes an essential ritual that must not be broken because it is perceived as necessary to survival.

Preparing to help

Before you seek to help a person with an eating disorder consider your own attitudes to body image, health, exercise, eating and weight

Helping to manage a situation in which a student has an eating disorder could well involve most if not all of the following:

- ❒ Consulting other members of the pastoral team
- ❒ Approaching the student
- ❒ Talking to the parents
- ❒ Dealing with the concerns of fellow students

Often a mixture of these responses may be appropriate. You might not be the best person to help the student deal with her problems, but you could be an essential link in finding her the support she needs.

The most valuable personal preparation is to have some factual knowledge of the problems, such as that outlined on pages 9 to 16. A word of warning: Consider your own attitudes to body image, health, exercise, eating and weight before you take any action.

Consulting other members of the pastoral team

The earlier an eating disorder is identified and dealt with, the better the hope of recovery

Eating disorders may cause students to be irrational in their thoughts and actions. They may also be resistant to help from other people. It is important, before approaching the student, to discuss the issue with another member of staff, and to outline the approach you are planning to take. This may also help you decide if the problem might be better dealt with by someone else.

It is important that the situation is shared in this way because further problems may arise. As with other pastoral care issues, details of one-to-one discussions probably need to be noted and a copy kept in the student's confidential file. Guidelines on this may vary from school to school.

Approaching the student

Friends and teachers are often in a better position than family to notice, acknowledge and act on early signs of eating disorders. This is important because the earlier an eating disorder is identified and dealt with, the better the hope of recovery.

Encourage the student to talk with the school nurse or her doctor; offer to accompany her to seek further help

It is usually best at first to avoid confronting the issue directly. One way is to arrange a 'routine' school medical examination (with the parents' permission) and to discuss the results. Another is to express your concern about specific issues - underachievement, incomplete work, poor health, unhappiness, conflict with teachers or with other students. The conversation may then lead more naturally towards the eating disorder.

If there is no initial response, make it clear that you have a strong feeling that something is wrong. Say that you are willing to talk further and that you care enough to check later about how things are going.

At some point you may feel it appropriate to confront the issue more directly. If you do so:

❒ Be honest
❒ Be compassionate
❒ Express willingness to obtain more information, if needed, and to talk further
❒ Encourage the student to talk with the school nurse or her doctor; offer to accompany her to seek further help
❒ Avoid commenting on the girl's weight or how she looks, as this may be misinterpreted and have unintended effects. Instead, concentrate on how the eating disorder may be affecting other aspects of her life

It is helpful to have another staff member present when confronting the issue directly (see page 27, 'Working with the student to adjust personal goals').

Talking to the parents

Don't treat her differently from the rest of the class or give her special attention unless it is really necessary

Depending on the circumstances, if an eating disorder is suspected it may be advisable for a senior member of the pastoral team or the headteacher to consult with the parents. They may be able to provide details from the doctor about the student's general health, and general advice about meals and how to treat her.

Such guidelines are likely to involve the following:

- ❒ Don't treat her differently from the rest of the class or give her special attention unless it is really necessary
- ❒ If she feels ill, get her to lie down for an hour and then encourage her to continue with the rest of the day if possible
- ❒ Urge her to eat a balanced school meal, even if only in small portions. Alternatively, she may wish to bring a packed lunch. If the school can offer direct supervision, see that she is challenged when she makes excuses for not eating: headache, tummy ache, feeling sick, extra work, music practice, looking for lost property
- ❒ Encourage her to keep normal school hours and to hand in work on time, even if she hasn't completed it. She may tend towards perfectionism, but don't allow her to rework assignments over and over again as she strives to achieve

Direct confrontation of parents can often lead to denial and a spoiling of the relationship between parents and school. It is also a fact that having a family member with an eating disorder creates many new and unfamiliar problems and challenges. With this in mind it is useful to give parents the address of the Eating Disorders Association and to keep a selection of books on the subject for loan or purchase. See pages 38 to 40 for details of these.

Dealing with the concerns of fellow students

If fellow students approach you with their concerns, be careful to respect the privacy of the person under discussion

Sometimes fellow students may alert you to a person with an eating disorder. The following guidelines are useful in such cases:

- ❒ Be approachable and understanding
- ❒ Be careful to respect the privacy of the person under discussion
- ❒ Try to understand their concern, confusion, lack of knowledge or fear of betraying a friend
- ❒ Remain patient, supportive and available

Working with the student to adjust personal goals

The extent to which you may be able to help a student will depend on:

- The student's individual circumstances
- The mechanisms in school for support and supervision of students with such problems
- Time constraints and your commitments to other students

Once medical help has been sought, much of the work is likely to be done by a therapist or counsellor. It may be necessary, in conjunction with this, for a member of the pastoral staff or the form tutor to help the student take an inventory of stress factors in her life. These can involve every area of school life - academic work, sport, music, hobbies, responsibilities, amount of homework, friends or lack of them. It may also be desirable to discuss aspects of life outside school.

Eating disorders often occur against a background of the person feeling pressured by school and/or parents

Eating disorders often occur against a background of the person feeling pressured by school and/or parents. Consider using the following, though remember that teachers need to set their own boundaries as to which elements to include:

- ❒ Evaluate together the student's personal limitations and help her to accept them
- ❒ Explore with her the possibility of change without her feeling guilty or inadequate
- ❒ Help her to set realistic goals and to escape from the perfectionist's performance trap
- ❒ Advise her that all projects involve risk-taking and help her to find confidence in facing the possibility of failure
- ❒ Give her as much responsibility as possible for her own choices and freedom to express herself
- ❒ Acknowledge and affirm sexuality as good. (Sexual feelings tend to decrease as weight gets lower and emotions in general become less strong)

During such discussions bear in mind that eating disorders are accompanied by altered thinking, especially if weight is dropping (see pages 19 and 20).

Family background

Dynamics within the family may have contributed to the condition

Dynamics within the family may have contributed to the condition. It is sometimes possible to look at areas that have been difficult and to understand how they relate to the eating disorder. At the same time it must be emphasised that *all* families have some problems, and parents must not be blamed.

Possible problem areas include:

In some families, children must measure up to set standards. The child learns: 'I'm unacceptable if I'm not perfect.'

1. Lack of family communication

This can include difficulty in dealing openly and honestly with basic issues and the unusual stresses of life. Deep feelings are not expressed and conflict is avoided in favour of maintaining a calm exterior. Self-sacrifice is highly prized.

The child learns: 'I should deny my needs and feelings.'

2. Great emphasis on academic and social achievement

Children here must measure up to set standards.

The child learns: 'I'm unacceptable if I'm not perfect.'

3. An over-involved family not giving the chance for growth

Parents' own disappointments with careers or relationships may become 'unfinished business' passed on to the child. Here, control of children by making them feel guilty is considered acceptable.

The child learns: 'My thoughts and feelings don't count.'

4. Food used by a girl as a way of controlling the family; mealtimes become a place of tension and conflict

Parents believe that the child is responsible for their own anger.

The child learns: 'I should hide all my anger.'

5. A parent physically or emotionally absent

When a parent is physically or emotionally absent, the child learns: 'I'm not important. Feelings and longings are wrong.'

For instance, the father may travel a great deal or the mother is depressed or suffering from an addiction. Family members may be expected to take care of themselves; nurturing and affection are seen as unnecessary or wrong.

The child learns: 'I'm not important. Feelings and longings are wrong.'

6. Traumatic events such as sexual, physical or emotional abuse have occurred or may be ongoing

The faulty conclusions a child makes may produce more than one pattern of defensive behaviour. This is developed subconsciously for survival and to avoid further pain. Such self-protection leads to other problems, too. These include an abnormal desire to please people, inability to cope with painful situations, inability to have a sense of separate identity, and false guilt.

The child learns: 'It's my fault when bad things happen.'

Teachers as carers

Exercise great care and sensitivity in dealing with family issues. Each school has its own procedure for communicating with parents. These, and the family's right to privacy, must be respected.

Special skills are needed in helping a person whose behaviour is addictive or compulsive. Don't dwell on food and weight; encourage positive activities and attributes

Family, friends and youth workers may also be involved in providing support. It is important to check who is involved and to what extent. Many hours can be taken up by a needy person going from one listener to another. On the other hand, there is a lot of advantage in planned sharing of support; people with eating disorders are likely to need help over a long period of time.

The approach must be non-condemning. It needs to have appropriate boundaries, such as times for talking things through. The teacher will provide information but will not make decisions for the person concerned. This shows the girl that she is responsible for her own choices and decisions.

Special skills are needed in helping a person whose behaviour is addictive or compulsive. Don't dwell on food and weight; encourage positive activities and attributes.

An isolated person in a caring role can be in danger either of over-indulgence or of being manipulated

Teachers involved in this caring work need support themselves. They need the full backing of others. An isolated person in a caring role can be in danger either of overindulgence or of being manipulated. Be willing to admit when you are out of your depth and need to engage extra help.

Look after yourself as well as caring for others. Eat healthy food, take exercise, spend time with friends.

When medical help is sought

Medical treatment for an anorexic or bulimic aims to restore the person to a weight acceptable for maintaining good health through eating an adequate balanced diet. It also seeks to help her to relinquish habits of bingeing, vomiting and/or purging. In many cases of obesity it is considered healthier for children to grow in height and maturity without increasing in weight rather than having to submit to a dieting regime.

Treatment to help psychological readjustment will often be needed. This is because resolution of some of the internal conflict is essential if the physical aspects of anorexia, bulimia or compulsive eating are to be resolved in a lasting way.

Some family doctors are themselves able to treat the person with an eating disorder. This is especially effective if they have a community psychiatric nurse, counsellor and dietician, who can give more specific advice and support. Other doctors will opt to refer the patient to a psychiatrist.

Outpatient treatment

An anorexic will generally attend a clinic on a weekly basis and will be seen by a doctor or psychiatrist and a dietician. She may be required to join a support group. Usually there will be provision for family support. Bulimics can also be helped effectively through outpatient clinics, particularly if they are of normal or above normal weight. Such help for bulimics, however, is not yet widely available through the National Health Service.

Admission to hospital

Results are better when the person agrees to being admitted to hospital and is treated as an individual accountable for her own actions

Most hospital admissions for eating disorders are made to psychiatric wards. This follows a period of outpatient treatment which enables the unit to thoroughly assess the patient. She will then be asked to sign an agreement to comply with the programme.

Results are better when the person agrees to being admitted to hospital and is treated as an individual accountable for her own actions. Sometimes, emergency treatment may be needed for complications caused by very low weight. In these cases the patient may be treated in a general hospital and fed intravenously or through a stomach tube in order to safeguard her life. Once above her critical weight, the patient can be transferred to a psychiatric ward for specialised help.

In hospital there may be psychotherapy, group work, occupational and art therapy and perhaps family therapy

There the anorexic will be set a target weight to be reached over a specified period of time. She will be given a set diet, increasing as soon as possible to 3000 calories a day. In the early stages there will also be limitations on her physical activity. The aim is to enable her to reach a weight at which she begins to think more accurately and can make good use of psychotherapy.

As the patient gains weight she is given more privileges. She is allowed to stay up for longer periods, have more visitors and can go out of hospital for a few hours. The anorexic understands that if she fails to make progress she may not be allowed to continue on the programme. If she wants the support provided she will seek to work within the guidelines. As her acceptable behaviour is rewarded, she moves away from her introverted and often manipulative behaviour.

In hospital there may be psychotherapy, group work, occupational and art therapy and perhaps family therapy. Group work helps the patient become able to talk about her self-discovery, to accept help and to begin helping others. Family therapy enables family members to discover the effects of their behaviour on others. It also helps both family and patient to see that life need not revolve around one person with problems.

Before being discharged, the patient will have trial periods at home.

Outpatient support and follow-up

> The person with an eating disorder may need ongoing care for up to four years

The person with an eating disorder may need ongoing care for up to four years. This is arranged through attending outpatient clinics. Taking part in a community support group is also encouraged. Funding for follow-up work depends on the local health authority. Voluntary support is available through such groups as the Eating Disorders Association and Anorexia & Bulimia Care (see addresses on page 40).

Is there hope?

A person with an eating disorder can recover fully, provided that there is no permanent damage to the bones or the reproductive system. Sadly, such damage sometimes occurs in anorexia. It is also a fact that many anorexics, while appearing to recover, have in fact changed to bulimia.

For a person to recover fully, the problems in emotions and thought patterns need to be dealt with. Only then can there be hope of a permanent change in behaviour

For a person to recover fully, the problems in emotions and thought patterns need to be dealt with. Only then can there be hope of a permanent change in behaviour.

A girl who recovered describes what happened: 'I was miserable and depressed to the point of wanting to end it all. My whole life was a farce as I refused to let anyone know about my anorexia. I was surviving on one or perhaps two apples a day. There were times when I was unsure if I could put one foot in front of the other.' She went on to seek help of various kinds until she found a counsellor. 'My counsellor helped me to look not just at the anorexia but at the thought processes hidden behind it. I'd always thought that if I were slim, people would like me and approve of me more. I'd had problems with friends at school because I always demanded a lot from them. I felt everything should be done perfectly, and I had high expectations when it came to exams.'

In addition to her emotions and thoughts, the *spiritual* part of her personality needed caring for. 'I began to see that the only way to have security and a sense of worth was through God. He created me and he knew what I needed. It was Easter and, although I was still afraid of the anorexia, I asked God to take charge of my life. Although recovery was not immediate, I began to believe that I could change. I could get rid of the past and develop a self-concept based on God's unconditional love and acceptance.

'My eating is now completely normal again, and my weight is just right for my height'

'I've always been distant from my dad because he was busy at his job or with voluntary work. We had a communication problem. I learned to forgive him, and that forgiveness released me to forgive others. On the other hand, I was overdependent on my mum, and I've had to learn to stand on my own two feet.

'I now have real friendships with both my parents. Best of all, my eating is now completely normal again, and my weight is just right for my height.'

Helpful books and publications

Beyond Chaotic Eating, Helena Wilkinson, Hodder & Stoughton, 1993
A well set out and comprehensive book that looks at the nature and causes of all three eating disorders. Options for help are described in detail.

Anorexia Nervosa and the Wish to Change, Crisp, Joughin, Halek, Bowyer
A self-help book written by medical staff at St George's Hospital, London. Available from the Eating Disorders Association (see page 40).

Bulimia Nervosa: A Guide to Recovery, Peter J Cooper, Robinson Publishing, 1993
A self-help book by a lecturer in psychopathology at Cambridge University. He runs a National Health clinic for bulimics.

Puppet on a String, Helena Wilkinson, Hodder & Stoughton, 1984
A personal experience of recovery from anorexia.

Dying to be Thin, Elizabeth Round, Lion Publishing, 1990
A pocket-sized book explaining how eating disorders can start from dieting. It explains the disorders and their causes as well as practical steps towards recovery.

Anorexia: The Broken Circle, Ann Erichsen, Faber & Faber, 1985
A useful book including specific guidelines for parental involvement in the healing process.

Surviving an Eating Disorder, Siegel, Brisman & Weinshel, Harper Row, 1988
A guide for friends and relatives about overcoming helplessness and taking action. Includes advice on what to say and what not to say.

Nutritional Medicine, Stephen Davies & Alan Stewart, Pan Books, 1987
An excellent book in basic nutrition for reading and reference, written by doctors who specialise in nutritional medicine.

Beat Premenstrual Tension with Diet, Maryon Stewart, Ebury Press, 1990
Based on the unique approach of the Women's Nutritional Advisory Service, which is medically backed by Dr Alan Stewart

Most of the above books can be obtained from:

Family Reading Centre Ltd
126 Sutherland Avenue
Biggin Hill
Kent TN16 3HJ
Telephone: 0959-575172 Fax: 0959-576445

Useful organisations

Eating Disorders Association

Sackville Place
44 Magdalen Street
Norwich NR3 1JE   Telephone: 0603-621414

Offers an information pack, including booklists, news about research projects, details of local self-help groups and support for parents.

Anorexia and Bulimia Care

Southern office:
Arisaig
Back Lane
Monks Eleigh
Suffolk IP7 7BA

Northern office:
15 Fernhurst Gate
Aughton
Ormskirk
Lancashire L39 5ED

A Christian-based organisation providing information, newsletters and a network of people in churches willing to befriend young people with eating disorders.

Women's Nutritional Advisory Service

PO Box 268
Hove
East Sussex BN3 1RW   Telephone: 0273-771366

Provides nutritional information about treatment of premenstrual stress, often helpful for girls and women who are bulimics or compulsive eaters.